Wine I Business Startup

How to Start, Run, and Grow Your Own successful Wine importing Business from Home

By

George A. Stewart

In This Book

Introduction

When I first began studying wine, a clever old man once advised me always to spin the bottle around and pay attention to the importer.

His reasoning was that, if you savored a particular wine, there was a great possibility you'd appreciate other wines from the same selection or importer. This suggestion helped me considerably in the initial years of my wine business.

I soon discovered how to follow the labels that bore the names Rosenthal, Lynch, Chatterton, and Wasserman. These were the wines that I personally most enjoyed. I must have good taste in wine!

Distribution is mainly hidden from the end customer. Labels and portfolios swap their loyalty all the time.

That import brand by law is part of the labeling and packaging, which joins the quality of a particular wine with the character and ultimately the reputation of the importer.

The last decade has witnessed an increase of small to mid-sized importers who have set up shop across the country.

Why the vertical shift? It could be an industry acknowledgment of the widespread stabilization of American shipping houses, with smaller labels becoming forgotten in the shuffle and striving for a more informal type of image.

It could additionally be due to the clear increase in—and demand for—boutique styles of production from across the globe, primarily outside of traditional realms.

It could also very well be this: when contrasted to other industry businesses that import wine, the obstacle to entry in the industry is a little less daunting.

A wine import business is one that requires low startup funds and but has a high-profit margin.

If you prefer versatility and want to quit your 9 to 5 job, then you should contemplate starting your own wine import business.

The great thing about this kind of market is that you can decide when and how to operate. The fact that wine is generally consumed by people of all backgrounds and classes makes it a viable and lucrative business.

The method of operating this kind of business is easy. But if you really want to make it in this type of business, you must possess good marketing and managerial abilities.

With wine imports, you won't have to worry about production costs or the core advertising cost. Your only worry will be how to create more distribution channels for your wine.

Create contacts with multiple wine production companies to distribute their products, and you will make great returns on your investment.

If in fact, your desire is to make good returns on your investment, then it is imperative that you conduct a comprehensive market survey. You will identify areas where you can distribute your wine. You'll also identify the brand of wine that is selling well in your selected market.

During your market survey, you would have to talk to owners of groceries stores, liquor stores, bars, country clubs, and anywhere wine is sold in your selected market. You'll gather information about the brands of wine they need to fill their wine racks and the amount they would be willing to pay.

This will guide you to know the type of wine production companies to align with. Knowledge obtained through your market survey will enable you to create effective distribution channels.

Apart from the initial product investment, the fees are extremely reasonable. Having a warehouse or brick-and-mortar building is not a legal requirement to operate in most of the United States.

It is quite possible, at least in the beginning, to manage the workload solely. Certainly, several of today's biggest and most influential import labels began that way - as home-based startups and solo operations.

If you are serious about starting your own wine distribution company, this book will ensure you are well equipped to handle the challenge.

Chapter Overview

In "Starting a Wine Importing Business Basics," we will kick things off by discussing the paperwork issues of starting a wine importing business.

As with any business you operate, you want to make sure you have all of your legal documentation and basic structure in place before you actually start importing or selling wines. We will go over all of that in more detail during this chapter.

Even businesses that operate as home-based businesses need to have a solid business plan. I will provide you with detailed tips and ideas for writing a compelling and effective business plan so you can expand your wine importing business.

Then we will go into how to create an online presence and market your wine import business according to legal statutes. The same three bureaus that regulate the alcohol and tobacco industry also set codes for how alcoholic beverages can be marketed to the public.

Once we have gotten all of the housekeeping paperwork out of the way, it's time to talk more about legalities and compliance.

In "Wine Import/Export Regulations," we'll discuss the federal agencies that are involved in these business practices.

We will go over the major agencies with which you must comply and what licenses and permits you will need to obtain before you can start importing wine.

In this section, we will go into an explanation of the common terms of sale used in wine importing transactions, as well as the duties and taxes imposed on wine from the government.

"Getting Started with Wine Imports" is where things get exciting.

Now that you have the legal requirements in place, it's time to move on to the next step and lay the foundation for the starting your shop. That requires obtaining the right software and establishing the proper infrastructure to help you manage and eventually grow your wine importing business.

The "Profit and Growth" chapter will give you the tools you need to keep your business thriving – and in the black.

Next, we will discuss how to private label your wine business. I'll show you how to do it correctly to avoid the most common mistakes new entrepreneurs make when private labeling their wine.

In "Expanding to Multiple States," we will discuss how to stay competitive and relevant in an ever increasing and strongly regulated market.

This is the time after you have grown your portfolio to the point where the expansion makes sense. It is recommended that you do not try to accomplish this alone.

In the chapter titled, "Standing out from the Crowd," we will step back from the rule of law. We will examine building the character of your business in order to stay relevant.

You've come a long way to build your portfolio and expand, now it's time to work on standing out from the crowd.

As a bonus, in the glossary, I've included a list of the state by state wine shipping laws as a reference to help you get started.

Beginning Business Basics

A wine import business is an endeavor that you can begin whether you are a total newbie to the industry or have been personally importing wine for years.

The stark contrast between wine importing as a business model compared to a traditional retail setting leads to the ease of starting a wine import business.

This industry is highly regulated. As daunting as that may seem, the reward is that you are under the same protections of federal and state laws as anyone you conduct business with. That means anyone you choose to do business with must also be properly licensed and bonded.

The wine import business is extremely lucrative because you can essentially run the entire business without ever hiring a single staff person or scouting an expensive warehouse location.

Running the business on your own allows you to establish personal relationships with vintners in your local area. They will know you and hopefully, also want to form a relationship with you as well.

Before we get into the basic paperwork, it's important we talk about the type of documentation you are going to need. That documentation is dependent upon the capacity for which you choose to operate.

You will need to know whether you want to establish yourself as a company or if you are required to do so. There's a thin line between personally importing and the need for obtaining licensure and registration with your state.

This may sound completely odd considering this book is about starting a wine-importing business, but let's discuss whether or not you even need to register a company. It's best if you consider this now rather than after you have invested a lot of time and money.

This decision is based on a few considerations. How big do you plan on making this operation? Will you be able to really see a profit consistently based on what you say you can sell?

If the amount is less than $75,000, then it might be worth considering going the hobbyist route instead of forming a full-blown business or working under the label of an existing distributor.

You can also work with dealers who only deal with consignments. There are tons of creative ways to avoid the traditional overhead of a standard business.

The Customs Border Protection Agency determines how much you can personally import before obtaining a license and permit.

If running a thriving, multi-state wine import business is going to be your ultimate goal, then you will need to be familiar with a ton of rules and regulations. Once you have registered in your local state, there are established laws that include the regulation of taxes and fees.

It's also notably important that you will be entering into a liability agreement with the United States government as an importer.

Simply put, when you import items into the U.S., you become wholly liable for whatever happens as a result of the distribution and consumption of those products by the public.

When you first begin your business, there are some key people whom you may want to consider including in the process.

These important professionals are:

- A lawyer
- An accountant
- A Custom's broker agent

While you will be running the business yourself, there are several tasks that are essential to be established as a company. These key players can be effective in assisting you with completing these important tasks.

Below I have listed the most critical and necessary documents that every single wine import business must have executed prior to your first acquisition or importing your first shipment.

First, let's take a look at how much it's going to cost you to start.

Estimated Start-up Costs

The cost of purchasing a vineyard and building facilities continues to increase. In addition, persevering through the lengthy and complicated permitting process can cause more frustration than a glass of wine can cure.

Rather than planting your own vineyard, you can simply choose to import and sell that beautiful wine created by others.

Some of the required resources listed in this table will be discussed at length later in this book. Here is an initial outline of the estimated costs to begin this wine import company:

Cost	**Resource**
FREE	Federal Basic Permit
Varies By State	Home State LLC Registration
It is dependant on the taxes and duties you have paid during the past year.	Customs Continuous Bond
% of Back-end profits	Logistics

$0 Set up Fee	White Labeling
$0 if You White Label/$up to $12,000	Wine Supplies
$500-$1,000	Marketing & Advertising
$1,000	Software/Equipment/Office Supplies/Internet Phone
FREE	FDA Product Registration
FREE	Certificate Label of Application (COLA)
FREE	EIN
$300 and $600 per hour (or a negotiated	Business Attorney

flat fee to do a task such as establishing an LLC)	
$150-$400 or more an hour, depending on the type of work	Accountant
A brokerage fee, which is usually determined as a percentage of the value of the imported shipment	Customs Broker

With as little as $500, you can start operating your business today and gradually work into the other expenses as you can afford to do so.

You should have a budget and method of acquisition for these expenses in your business plan.

A Business Plan

This is probably the number one most important step in forming any new business.

While I will admit, writing a business plan is not for the faint of heart, there are alternatives to having it prepared professionally.

There are plenty of templates available online for free or for a small fee. You could also choose to hire a business plan writer from sites like Upwork, Fiverr, or Freelancer.

The goal of a successful business plan is multifaceted. The key is to keep it simple. Just be clear and concise. Keep it short. No one is going to read hundreds of pages that you have slaved over.

Keep in mind the main goals of a business plan.

- It is a roadmap to the success of your business.
  - It is focused on reaching your financial and personal goals.

- It is a road map to obtaining financing.
  - It persuades others to invest in your dream.

Your business plan is important in order to identify and define your business' current standing and what your future goals, plans, and commitments are.

Where do you even start? Start with a cover page followed by a Table of Contents then go on from there.

The components of a Business Plan are outlined here:

- Executive Summary
  - Mission
  - Objectives
  - Keys to Success
- Company Summary
  - Company Ownership
  - Start-up Summary
- Services
  - Pricing and Profitability
- Market Analysis Summary
  - Market Segmentation

- o Target Market Segment Strategy
- Strategy and Implementation Summary
  - o Competitive Edge
    - Main Competitors
  - o Marketing Strategy
    - Marketing Program
  - o Sales Strategy
    - Sales Forecast
  - o Milestones
- Web Plan Summary
- Management Summary
  - o Management Team
- Personnel Plan
- Financial Plan
  - o Important Assumptions
  - o Break-even Analysis
  - o Projected Profit and Loss
  - o Projected Cash Flow
  - o Projected Balance Sheet
  - o Business Ratios
  - o Exit Strategy

You may also want to include a list of your suppliers or the wineries that you are working with (or wish to work with) or anything else that exhibits the validity of your business.

Some of these sections will be fairly easy to complete, especially if you're contemplating running things alone. In the Management Summary and Personnel Plan, you may plan to be the only employee and manage things yourself. That's all you need to indicate in these sections.

Remember to be concise, yet realistic, and truthful.

In another chapter, we will address marketing and advertising strategies, as this industry is highly regulated in that regard.

Be prepared to make changes to your business plan as you go along. You will learn much in the process, and a business plan is meant to be re-evaluated and revised as needed.

Employer Identification Number

You need an Employer Identification Number (EIN) from the IRS.

An EIN or Employer Identification number is essentially a social security or tax identification number for your business.

The IRS and many other governmental agencies can identify your business via this unique 9 digit number.

It is simple to apply for this number and either you can do it yourself or get your accountant to apply for you.

Fill out Form SS-4, which can be filed online, via Fax, or by mail.

Here is a link to the IRS website where you can download or complete the form online. https://www.irs.gov/businesses/small-businesses-self-employed/how-to-apply-for-an-ein

This number is required before you file your federal importer permit with the Alcohol and Tobacco Tax and Trade Bureau (TTB). This number is also required before you open a bank account for your company.

If your business is established as anything other than a sole proprietorship, you must obtain this from the IRS.

Basic Importer Permit

You need a federal basic importer permit with the TTB. You must apply for this permit in order to import wines to the U.S. The permit must be issued to your importing business at the address that is your place of business.

You can find this form here and complete it and submit it online.

https://www.ttb.gov/forms/f510024.pdf

You can read more information about the form and the TTB regulations about this form here:

https://ttb.gov/itd/importing_alcohol.shtml

Usually, it takes about 60 to 90 days for the federal importer permit to be granted.

You will need a letter from a winery (often called a Letter of Intent) indicating the promise on behalf of the winery to export wine to your company.

Wholesaler Application Form

You can find a complete list of the paperwork you will need to complete here on the U.S. Department of Treasury Alcohol and Tobacco Tax and Trade Bureau site.

This form can usually be combined with your importer permit when you apply for that with the TTB.

https://www.ttb.gov/applications/wholesaler_impor ter_packet.shtml

Certificate of Label Application (COLAs)

Once you obtain your basic importing permit, you should immediately apply for access to online submission of your labels to the Certificate of Label Application (COLA).

You can read more about applying for the COLA online here https://www.ttb.gov/labeling/colas.shtml or https://www.ttb.gov/labeling/colas-docs/create-an-application.pdf

This simple one-page form is provided free of charge.

It takes approximately 30 days to process.

This step ensures your online access is ready when you have labels to present.

FDA Product Registration

As an importer, you'll need to record a Food and Drug Administration (FDA) registration number from each supplier.

The suppliers should already have this number if they are shipping to the U.S.

If you are storing the wine at your own facility, you will also need to obtain this registration number.

The registration process is free.

More information may be found on the FDA's Registration of Food Facilities web page.
https://www.fda.gov/food/guidance-regulation-food-and-dietary-supplements/registration-food-facilities

Broker Power of Attorney

In order to have a customs broker act on behalf of an importer, a Broker Power of Attorney must be executed by an officer of the importing company.

This relatively simple document is a requirement. It is a fairly easy step to complete in the initial compliance process.

Example Broker Power of Attorney

You can read the federal statutes that indicate the necessity for a power of attorney to be filed with your customs broker agency here:

In order to serve and to act on your behalf as a U.S. Licensed Customs Broker, it is a requirement by Customs and Border Protection that brokers have a signed Power of Attorney on file prior to transacting in Customs business.

Note: Brokers can act on behalf of importers by clearing their cargo with U.S. Customs and Border Protection (CBP) as well as with other relevant government agencies such as the FDA and Bureau of Alcohol, Tobacco, Firearms, and Explosives (ATF).

Incorporate as a Business

Register your business with the state in which you plan on operating as well as any other states you plan to do business in.

One of the most rewarding experiences of registering a business is deciding what you will call it.

States are primarily concerned with their own borders, so incorporation of a wine import business in one state doesn't keep anyone from registering a wine import business with the same name in another state.

We will discuss registering with other states in the following section regarding "Foreign Registration."

When starting a business, there are five different business structures you can choose from:

- Sole Proprietor
- Partnership
- Corporation (Inc. or Ltd.)
- S Corporation
- Limited Liability Company (LLC)

A sole proprietorship is used for a business owned by a single person or a married couple.

Under this structure, the owner is personally liable for all business debts and may file business income and expenses on their personal income tax.

A partnership often requires an agreement between two or more individuals who are going to own and operate a business jointly.

The partners will share all aspects of the business in accordance with the agreement. Partnerships don't pay taxes, but they need to file an informational return.

Individual partners then report their share of profits and losses on their personal tax returns.

With a corporation, profits are taxed both at the corporate level and again when distributed to shareholders. When you structure a business at this level, there are often lawyers involved.

An S Corporation is one of the most popular types of business entities people form. This structure avoids double taxation.

It is taxed similar to a partnership entity, but an S Corp. needs to be approved to be classified as such.

A Limited Liability Company (LLC) is the most common business structure. It reduces the risk of losing all of your personal assets if you are faced with a lawsuit. It provides a clear separation between business and personal assets.

You can also elect to be taxed as a corporation, which saves you money come tax time.

If you are unsure which specific business structure you should choose, then you can discuss it with an accountant. They will direct you in the best possible option for what your business goals are.

Plan a Business Structure

Once you have your EIN, LLC or other business incorporation filed, and all of your paperwork in order, then it's time to get the final documents your business will need.

This next step includes gathering information and deciding on what you want your business model to be.

You need to document who owns the company with you, and who will be responsible for the management and operations of the company.

Generally, this document is called the "Articles of Incorporation (or Organization)" for your business.

This information will also be helpful in writing your business plan.

Here is an example of an Articles of Incorporation:

Open a Business Bank Account

This is one important step, but it can only be done after you have a fully executed article of incorporation which has been approved by the state, and you have an EIN number assigned by the IRS.

Once you have these two documents, you should be able to go to a bank and open your first commercial bank account.

Do your research and understand various types of commercial checking account fees. You will want to find a bank that offers free or an almost free commercial checking account.

Some larger banks can charge you hundreds of dollars each month depending on how many transactions you do.

Make sure to ask and shop around before you sign on the dotted line.

The bank will want to know in detail who owns the company, what percentage each person owns, and who is authorized to make purchases.

They may want to see a copy of your Business Plan, LLC documents, or Articles of Organization.

Call ahead to your preferred bank of choice for their requirements.

Foreign Registration

In the wine industry, if something wasn't created in that state, it could be considered foreign. The term "foreign" does not necessarily mean across the ocean or the world.

Each state behaves as if it exists independently from the rest of the country because states often get to make their own laws.

For example, if you form your company in New York, then New York is your domestic state or residence.

If you reside in New York but establish a business just across the bridge in New Jersey, it's considered to be a foreign company or LLC.

You will often hear it referred to as a "foreign business registration."

The term "foreign" does not mean it operates, was founded in, or resides outside of the United States. This term also applies to interstate commerce.

The constitution of the United States has made it so that all states must recognize equivalencies across state lines. If you form a company in South Carolina, it's valid in Virginia.

If you're a New York company doing business in New Jersey, then you have to complete a foreign registration in New Jersey. If you don't register, most states have some kind of penalty for you.

As far as the state is concerned, you don't exist unless you register with them.

The first step is ensuring you are registered in your home state as an LLC. You should have already completed this step if you are following along.

Secondly, contact the Secretary of State for the foreign state where you intend to conduct business. You can get a listing of the contact info for Secretaries of State here: http://www.statelocalgov.net/50states-secretary-state.cfm

Some states require you to include a copy of the original documents showing that the LLC has been registered in its "home" state, or a copy of the official document registering the LLC.

Tips for Running a Wine Import Business

We will go into more detail about establishing an online presence in the next chapter, but I'll start with the basics.

Create a Website

You will want to have a website built. A website should include valuable content about your wine selection, you as an owner, and your company information. It should also include a clearly stated Privacy Policy (as we will discuss in the "Marketing" chapter).

Without a web presence, there is no way for you to connect to international and interstate buyers and sellers. You don't necessarily have to run a brick and mortar warehouse for people to walk into, so your online presence is key.

Do Market Research

Take time to conduct extensive research about your chosen market. Investigate the climate of the industry to find out if there is a need for the type of wine you want to sell. This means you will also discover some of the barriers and risks involved with each target market.

Locate your competitors in the industry in your selected market. If you aren't finding any direct competition, then you need to keep digging and do more research. There is always competition out there, either directly or indirectly.

Develop Good Packaging

Take time to think about the packaging of your wine and the message you want to convey with it.

Creative packaging is what differentiates the good from the best.

Listen to your Customers

Determine the size of your operation. Listen to what your customers are telling you.

If you are constantly hearing that you have too wide a selection to choose from, that could be a problem. Too many choices often confuse people, and they wind up making no choice at all.

Trade Shows are Key

Take part in as many trade-shows in your area as possible. This gives you a way to offer wine tastings and face-to-face interactions about your label.

Trade shows may give you access to people who don't live locally and may be interested in having you ship their wine to them.

As you interact with these customers, it's important that you are knowledgeable about the wine you are selling. Be sure to respond quickly and honestly to their questions.

Describe your decision for choosing the flavors and combinations you chose. Be able to describe the reasons for the packaging design.

Tell them what your shipping and turnaround time is, what your fees consist of, and most importantly, what your expertise and credentials are that qualify you to be an expert in wine imports.

Talk to People!

If you get a chance to visit with customers in person, take it. Regular interaction with your local customers and vendors is a great way to personalize your relationship with them.

If you don't live near any of your customers, consider holding group video calls once or twice a month where you feature a new wine. Use it as an opportunity to educate your customers.

Customers and their satisfaction are the lifelines of any business, regardless of the industry or size.

In the wine industry, in particular, customer retention and referrals are a direct result of their satisfaction.

Why? Because in this industry, your customers, the ones who buy your wine, are anyone from an avid connoisseur, to a restaurant owner with multiple locations, to someone who has decided they want to join a wine of the month club and develop their pallet.

There is always someone out there willing to take your place if you aren't up to the task. Keep your customers returning, sending new business your way, and loyal to your brand by fully understanding what it is that has inspired them and how you can improve to raise the bar.

Acquire Strong Sales Leads

Find and keep strong sales leads. Take advantage of sales programs that are cost-effective and help you generate leads for your business.

Acquiring sales leads is a challenge that many businesses face, no matter the industry.

It is even more difficult when trying to enter into foreign markets. Here is where language barriers, customs, and sometimes even cultural differences are taken into consideration.

Plan for Change

If you don't remember anything else, remember this: a plan is just that - a plan.

It is up to you to actually execute it while simultaneously and consistently promoting your products and brand.

Be aware that change is consistent and to be expected.

Be prepared for changes in market shifts. Customer tastes and preferences may change, so be prepared.

Always be willing to alter your plans and even to edit your business plan as you gain experience.

Defining Terms of the Sale

It's critically important for all wine importers to understand their individual role when it comes to negotiating the terms of the sale with their suppliers.

I'm going to explain the most commonly used terms in the wine import industry.

Ex Works

The term "Ex Works" is used to describe the process of when you, as the seller, have a minimum obligation of storage and disposal transfer to the buyer, once they take possession of the wine. From that point, the buyer assumes the costs and risks associated with taking possession.

FOB

FOB stands for "free on board" or "freight on board."

This term is strictly used in the shipping industry. It is a designation that is used when you, as the seller, transfer ownership of your wine to the buyer.

It is merely used to determine which party will be responsible for paying the freight charges and at what specific point the ownership is transferred from you to the buyer.

CIF

You, as the seller, are responsible for paying the freight costs to bring the wine to the port of entry at a specified destination. That includes paying for insurance. At this point, the assumed risks are transferred to your buyer once the wine is loaded on a ship.

While these terms are not all inclusive of the wine importing industry terminology, they are the most important ones when it comes to the terms of the sale.

Digital Marketing According to Codes and Regulations

The alcohol industry is known for its Super-Bowl and Monday night football marketing campaigns. They are innovators at cultivating content on social media.

Despite the effortless ease with which big-name alcohol companies are able to get people to talk about and actually consume their brands, they are faced with the most rigid regulatory process. This process not only regulates selling alcoholic beverages but also in marketing and engaging with people who purchase it.

The Federal Trade Commission (FTC) has named the Beer Institute, the Distilled Spirits Council of the United States (DISCUS), and the Wine Institute as the regulatory agencies who adopt the marketing and advertising codes for the alcohol industry.

These marketing codes are constantly reviewed by the Federal Trade Commission.

These codes include strict guidelines about how to limit the chances of alcohol ads being specifically targeted towards under-age consumers.

For your particular business, you will want to become wholly familiar with the Wine Institute's "Digital Marketing Guidelines."

It could not hurt to review and become familiar with the other two codes as well.

Beer, Wine, and Spirits Marketing Guidelines

You can find links to the marketing codes, practices, and guidelines here:

Beer Institute Advertising and Marketing Code (https:/bit.ly/2kDOlWS)

DISCUS Code of Responsible Practices (https://bit.ly/2x4llPJ)

Wine Institute Digital Marketing Guidelines (https://bit.ly/2Y1Lmei)

The beer marketing code is as follows:

- Beer advertising should not suggest directly or indirectly that any of the laws applicable to the sale and consumption of beer should not be complied with.
- Brewers should adhere to contemporary standards of good taste applicable to all commercial advertising and consistent with

the medium or context in which the advertising appears.

- Advertising themes, creative aspects, and placements should reflect the fact that Brewers are responsible corporate citizens.
- Brewers strongly oppose abuse or inappropriate consumption of their products.

The DISCUS code includes:

- The responsible placement of advertising.
- Ads have responsible content.
- Responsibility with what their brand communicates.
- Marketing products to adults of legal purchasing age.
- All marketing conducted in an appropriate manner.

The wine code (which is most applicable to you as a wine import business) is as follows:

- Digital marketing communications are intended for adults of legal purchase age.
- Digital marketing communications should not be placed in media where more than 28.4%

of the audience is underage (determined by using reliable, up-to-date audience composition data).

- Digital marketing communications on a site or web page controlled by the brand advertiser that involve direct interaction with a user should require age affirmation by the user prior to full user engagement of that communication to determine that the user is of legal purchase age.

- User-generated content on a site or web page controlled by the brand advertiser should be monitored on a regular basis.

- Digital marketing communications that are intended to be forwarded by users should include instructions to individuals downloading the content that they should not forward these materials to individuals below the legal purchase age.

- Digital marketing communications on sites controlled by the brand advertiser must respect user privacy.

- Digital marketing communications and product promotions must be transparent as brand marketing by being identified as such.

The fundamental principles contained in any of the codes above can be broken down as follows:

- All digital marketing information will be designed for adults of legal buying age.
- All digital marketing information must be placed solely in communications and mediums, where more than 71% of the consumers of this information is of the legal purchase age.
- All digital marketing information that includes direct communication with a user must require age declaration prior to any engagement.
- All user-generated content on a website or webpage established by the brand must be policed and moderated on a routine basis.
- All digital marketing information that is intended to be transmitted or forwarded by users must include detailed instructions laying out that content must not and shall not be transmitted to anyone below the legal buying age.
- All digital marketing information must have the utmost respect for user privacy.

You can see how this is related to your business' marketing and advertising.

For clarity, let's dive a bit deeper into each of the main points of this code.

Most of this information is coming from a U.S. resident's perspective. You should research the rules and regulations of alcohol promotion in your country.

Social Media Prowess

When working with alcohol of any kind, and especially the complexities of wine, you need to know and understand your audience. This understanding is the first step to ensuring successful transmission of information to them.

It was reported in 2014 that more than 67% of the population in America of those age 12 and overuse social media. You can pretty much imagine that number is closer to 100% in 2019.

With that being said, it's extremely difficult for alcohol brands to promote and market effectively with minimal guarantees their ad will not reach someone under the legal buying age.

The average wine import business can select to advertise and market anywhere on social media; it still needs to be made clear that they are restricted to ONLY platforms where more than 70% of the content consumers are over the age of 21.

This imposes excruciating limits on the number of places and platforms that wine brands can effectively utilize to reach customers. It also forces them to do extensive research for each platform before they join.

When you engage in social media, it's like being a one-person consumer PR firm.

Your goal is to strike up a conversation about your wine importing business and present your clearly identified brand to the general public.

While it is necessary to still use traditional methods of advertising in print and online, for many home-based and smaller wine importers, the potential to reach a wider audience and the sheer economics that surround social media are quite compelling.

Does using social media really help you sell more wine?

Before there was a Facebook or Twitter, was it possible that media coverage, trade shows, and wine tasting events alone helped people sell more wine?

Does selling wine by any other method besides face to face sell wine?

There's no easy answer.

Marketing experts claim that it takes anywhere from 7 to 15 different touches before they become a new customer willing to purchase what you have to sell.

As a home-based wine importer, social media can help you attain those different touch points much faster than with the standard media marketing approaches.

It's called "social media" because it's 100% social interaction.

As a wine importing business, your social media should contain a mix of both information and promotional posts. The general rule is 80/20, respectively. That means you must establish some sort of credibility with the people who are going to consume your content before they even ask for it.

Most people won't even bother to ask, or even act until you ask them a question. It's called "call-to-action."

Be sure to include one, but no more than two, of these in each of your social media posts. It tells your content consumers what to do next, without leaving it up to them to figure out on their own.

An example is saying something like, "Be sure to leave a like!"

Don't just settle for traditional posts. If you want actually to have your content consumed, then you will need to have a small advertising budget for ads.

Big wineries, who advertise online regularly, understand that there are 3 types of people on social media:

- The people who can deliver impressions to your ads, also called "influencers."
- new followers
- potential customers.

There is a strong overlap between each type of online consumer.

You want to develop and nurture a strong working relationship with the influencers. That relationship is a great way to have your message amplified and to indirectly sell wine through social media advertising.

One vital mistake that many make is not being consistent with posts. Social media prowess is about consistently getting the right message out, to the right people, at the right time.

Think of social media as a long term strategy.

Platform-Specific Demographics

According to the Pew Internet Project's 2012 research conducted with American teens, more than

95% of children between the ages of 12–17 are online. 81% of them use some kind of social media.

Of those children, more than 77% of them use Facebook, and only 24% use Twitter.

There isn't a plethora of demographic data about children and pre-teens primarily, but more current analysis reveals that Instagram has grown very prevalent amid the adolescent generation.

According to eMarketer, 11.4 million of Instagram's 300 million members are age 17 or younger.

As of the spring of 2014, 30% of 12 to 17-year old's prefer Instagram, 27% and 23% favor Twitter and Facebook, respectively.

Age Confirmation

A very critical component in your research efforts is the definition of an adult.

For instance, Nielson has reported that as of 2014, over 71% of adults online are using Facebook.

It's important to note that the researchers are using the legal definition of as "adult" as someone being 18 years old. That doesn't help you as an alcohol brand here in the states, where the legal age is 21 for purchasing and consuming alcohol.

Fortunately, there is other data available from Nielson that shows more than 80% of the content consumers on Twitter, Facebook, and YouTube are over the age of 21.

Guaranteeing an audience over the legal buying age only gives you the legal right to create a profile and post to that account.

What it does not give you permission to do is to follow anyone, make a comment, or reply to their posts. This may seem a bit one-sided when trying to engage with your audience of potential buyers, vendors, and suppliers.

The only way to get around this snafu is enacting "age confirmation," which allows you to bypass this restriction on Facebook and Twitter.

Twitter

Twitter has an age-screening feature that requires individuals to present their date of birth in order to be able to follow an alcohol brand.

This feature is automatically triggered after an end-user clicks "Follow" on any alcohol brand's profile or page. The system will not let them proceed without entering a date of birth.

Twitter will then perform an algorithm check to ensure that the age entered matches the legal drinking age, based on the current date, the country where they live, and their account details.

Once the individual has been verified, then their "follow" status will be confirmed. If they do not pass, they will not be permitted to follow the page.

Twitter will remember that they did not meet those requirements, so there's no tricking the system. Just as equally, when you are verified, Twitter remembers you are of the legal drinking age. You don't have to go through the verification process to view the page again.

Facebook

Facebook restrictions work similarly, but the difference is they rely heavily on the date of birth entered when creating the profile as the basis for restriction verifications.

Underage consumers will not be able to view friends' likes or comments on alcohol-related pages, based on the date of birth in their profile.

It's equally as important for you to monitor the posts made to your business Facebook page.

Instagram

There is no way for anyone to verify their age on Instagram. That means alcoholic brands are restricted in the two-way engagement just like Twitter.

You can place a legal disclaimer in your bio to allow people to engage with you on other platforms. Guinness Beer, for example, does this very thing.

So, while you cannot follow anyone back or reply to anyone's comments on Instagram, many followers still choose to show brand loyalty with likes and comments on the brand's relevant posts.

Effectively Utilizing Social Media

Despite the restrictions and work around strategies, not all platforms are created equal when it comes to being effective for your business promotion and marketing campaigns.

It's important that you begin by creating a solid social media strategy prior to creating any new profiles or media channels.

For example, if your low hanging fruit is mostly men, you might want to consider having less of a presence on Pinterest, where the platform is dominated by the female demographic.

Likewise, if two-way communication and dialogue are critical to your brand and an integral part of your social media strategy, then it's safe to assume that Instagram is not the right choice for you.

If the demographics of the platform aren't matching up to your target audience, then there is no point in trying to make it work.

Hone Your Social Listening Skills

Most marketers are familiar with this important skill as it describes how efficient and effective it makes social engagement on social media.

It gives brands a general sense of how people are receiving their message and content.

The self-regulating guidelines state that alcohol brands must be responsible for and monitor content generated by their end users. This content must be appropriate and follow the rules for promoting responsible drinking among legal age buyers.

If you have any inappropriate content posted by followers, be sure to address it and remove it immediately.

You are not able to delete Tweets you didn't post, but you can remove comments and posts on Facebook, Instagram, and on your blog.

On Facebook, you can review each post made by users who interact with your page, prior to it being made public. This makes it easier for you to focus on the positive comments and responses you get.

End User Privacy

End-user privacy policies are put in place to help govern the dissemination and collection of our personal information. This policy is important for your website.

If you're going to be collecting information about your customers in any capacity, you must enact this privacy policy. This includes asking customers to be a part of an email list, whether or not they are making a purchase.

The DISCUS Guidelines (shared above) state that any alcoholic brand advertising online must have the following privacy policies in place and in writing.

"Prior to the collection of any information, the brand will require an individual to affirm that he or she is of legal purchase age, and user information can only be collected from those individuals who are of the legal purchase age."

"The brand shall employ a mechanism for a person to opt in before receiving a direct digital marketing communication and opt out to discontinue receiving direct communications."

"Clear information must be provided about collection and use of personal data. Under no circumstances will the information collected be sold or shared with third parties unrelated to the brand."

"People should be encouraged to read the privacy statement before submitting their information."

"Measures will be taken to keep user information secure and protected from loss or theft."

The liquor maker, Bacardi, has set a prime example of complete transparency in their privacy policy. They have a clear and concise online policy that is prominently displayed and linked to their Facebook page "about" section.

Wine Import/Export Regulations

Any beverage that contains alcohol falls under the purview of three Federal Bureaus or Agencies: The Alcohol and Tobacco Tax and Trade Bureau, the Food and Drug Administration, and the Customs and Border Protection agency.

Let's examine the requirements for importing wine into the United States since this is one of the major components of our "Import" business.

The alcohol and tobacco industry laws are regulated with extreme caution on both the federal and state level. In order for you to be legally able to import wine, you must comply with these requirements at both levels.

To make it easier for wine importers in general, I've gathered some general information for you to investigate further on your own.

This comes from my personal experience with working in the wine import industry. I will guide you through the regulations and sort through the confusing information.

If you can afford to do so, I highly recommend that you work with a professional or consultant who can provide you with direct insight into your business structure, wine choices, import basics, and operational guidance.

There are several individual agencies you are going to have to interact with. I've provided the documents you will need from these agencies in a previous chapter.

Let's talk about what they actually regulate and what their function will be as it relates to your wine import business.

The TTB

The Alcohol and Tobacco Tax and Trade Bureau (TTB) is a federal agency that comprises a large part of the government's Department of Treasury division. This organization is primarily responsible for the regulation of alcohol and tobacco production, imports, and distribution within the United States.

For those who import products, the TTB is the body that regulates the licensing needed based on what's being imported. They apply the appropriate duties, taxes, labeling, fees, and formulation of the product in question.

This is not a complete list of what they regulate, but it is important when knowing how to interact with them.

Before you can begin to even import under your brand to the United States commerce market, you must have labels that are approved by the TTB. That means, there is a federal process for getting your label approved.

You file this with your permit and the governing body will either reject, approve, or return your label with "corrections needed." This is the COLA process we discussed in the chapter regarding "Business Basics."

This does not apply to typical table wines, but it can be applied to specific imported wines depending on their class and type.

The FDA

Despite what you may believe or have been told, the Food and Drug Administration (FDA) does not have legal jurisdiction over alcoholic beverages in all cases.

For you, as an importer, this is important because one of your main considerations is complying with registration in accordance with the 2002 Bioterrorism Act.

That means that any company or facility that is responsible for manufacturing, processing, packaging, or holding food (yes, even wine), for human or animal consumption within the boundaries of United States, must be legally registered with the FDA.

As a wine importer, if you are going to work with a company to handle logistics and warehousing as you work from home, you need to make sure they are registered with the FDA.

If you are doing this on your own, you need to provide prior written notice to the FDA on all shipments for any type of food or beverage within the states.

The USCBP

The U.S. Customs and Border Protection (USCBP) agency will be the very first stop your wine makes when it reaches the country.

Customs and Border enforcement works closely with the TTB and the FDA to ensure that all items released to the public for consumption are of regulatory compliance.

They check that all standards are met and that the label has been approved by the federal government, which we referred to above as "COLA," from the TTB.

You'll also need to obtain a corresponding winery facility number, generated by the FDA, for the winery who will house your imports.

Licensure and Permits

While there is a lot to take into consideration when deciding to start a wine import business, there is help available, and it doesn't require a lot of money to get it.

Using outside consultants who specialize in compliance for importing wine is the best decision when starting out to ensure you stay and remain in compliance.

You don't need to keep them on retainer continually, but working with professional consultants in this area is often times a much more cost-effective way of doing business than trying to go it alone.

In some states, you will be required to be listed as the "Primary American Source" or to provide a letter called an "Appointment Letter." Please check with your local business registrar when obtaining your license to see if this is a requirement in your state.

You will need to obtain label approval or "COLA" for each wine you are planning on importing into the states.

Each of the labels that are on a bottle of imported wine must comply with regulations.

These regulations insist on these components to be listed on wine labels:

- clearly identifying a health warning
- declaration of present sulfites
- the entirety of net contents in metric form
- Brand name
- Class and Type designation
- Alcohol content
- Appellation of Origin

- Bottler's Name and Address

Every container of wine must have a brand name.

As was discussed in Chapter 1, it can take up to 30 days or more to get COLA approved, which is another reason to work with consultants to ensure that you meet all TTB requirements and deadlines.

Some states have regulations that restate and emphasize the basic federal requirement that wine labels may not create any erroneous impressions about the wine.

Each state's requirements are different and should be thoroughly reviewed to ensure compliance.

Professional consultants in the industry strategically align themselves with both federal and state agencies that are responsible for the regulation of food and alcohol.

They are more than generally familiar with each of the requirements and can help walk you through the entire process and the required procedures. Some of them are even capable of helping you file the basic permit application and all state-related licensure.

In addition, they can help you with label submission, paying taxes and duties, or just merely answering general questions about compliance or the terms of sale.

Equally important are the duties and taxes you need to pay on your imports.

Duties and Taxes

Before we dive into what those duties and taxes are, I want to familiarize you with a term called "duty-free shop."

These types of specialty shops can be found at airports, on international borders, and even on cruise ships. The items you can purchase from a duty-free shop are already priced to eliminate the customs duty taxes in a particular country.

That does not mean that you don't have to pay those custom duties or taxes in your local state of residence; in fact, you most certainly do.

For example, a US resident who buys two liters of alcohol in a duty-free shop at London's Heathrow Airport will pay less than the United Kingdom market price for those items. This is because the Value Added Tax (VAT) and any applicable UK customs duty will not be included in the sales price.

The duty-free shop will package that US resident's purchase in a way that prevents the US resident buyer from consuming the alcohol while still in the airport.

When you get back to the United States, you will need to complete a form that lists all of the items you brought back with you from your travels. Part of this declaration involves stating the value of the goods you obtained.

If the value of the goods combined exceeds the personal exemption you are given as a courtesy; you will then have to make a payment of the customs duties and taxes on anything in excess.

In the US, customs regulations declare that any adult over 21 years old is permitted to bring a maximum of 1 liter of alcohol into this country without paying any duty fees on it, no matter where it was originally bought.

The personal limit for duty-free items is $800.

If you live in a state with a port of entry that has more stringent restrictions on imports, those rules take precedence over any other regulations previously established. You may have to pay even more in taxes if that's the case.

Please be sure to check the country alcoholic beverage import policies and procedures prior to leaving home. It might not be worth the trip.

Write down all the prices for the local wines that you want to bring back to the States with you. Make sure to keep that list with you when you visit the shops you plan to purchase from.

This will ensure you are able to see if there are discounts and duty-free shops available, enough to help you save money and make a profit, even if you do have to pay any customs duties and taxes when you get back home.

Wholesale Laws

In the importing business, there are people who serve as the middle-tier to the 3 tier system.

They are referred to as "wholesalers" or "distributors." These people are licensed and pre-authorized to buy wine from an importer like yourself, for reselling on their own terms. This can include reselling it to the bottom tier, which includes restaurants, liquor stores, and bars.

It's important you determine what role you want to play in the wine import business.

Do you want to be just an importer, perhaps an agent of a local winery, do you want to do both? Do you want to be an importer and a wholesaler?

Ask yourself if you merely want to sell wines to individuals or do you also want to sell them to retailers.

Many wine importers choose to become both in some form, acting as a wholesaler and distributor for local wineries, and as an importer for foreign wineries.

An importer, not a wholesaler or distributor, has the following general responsibilities:

- Transparent and open communication with all foreign wineries.
- Receipts provided for all purchases.
- Arrange shipment and delivery by air or by sea from a foreign winery. This can be done directly or indirectly through a trusted freight forwarder.
- Clearance from customs once the wine has arrived in the US.
- Transportation arrangements for the transport of the wine from customs to a license and bonded warehouse facility located near the port, designed specifically for the storage of wine.
- Wholesale and retail outlet location selection.
- Promoting the sale of the brand through promotion and marketing.

A solely an importer, you have more control over how your brand manages and distributes the wine. Wholesalers and distributors, on the other hand, don't have as much control.

Consider that in order for you to be able to import wine from certain foreign countries, you will need to obtain a special certification that shows you have all the proper procedures and practices in place in the manufacturing country of origin.

There are also requirements that must be met by the 2004 TTC (Trade and Technical Corrections) Act.

This certification from the country of origin contains a specific statement from the manufacturer's government, containing the results of analysis and lab work that was conducted on the wine, including what cellular treatments were employed.

Most of the international agreements in place surrounding trade have excluded some countries from this strict requirement. You can find all of the countries who are exempt from certification requirements on the TTB website.

For example, if you live in New York, you will be required to obtain the "Wholesaler's Basic Permit" from the TTB, as well as a Wholesaler Application from the ABCC (Alcoholic Beverages Control Commission).

An applicant for an importer's simple permit who also needs to submit an application as a wholesaler no longer needs to apply for these permits separately.

Instead, the applicant may indicate a cause to be both an importer and wholesaler.

That is an alternative only for those people who could be importing to and dispensing from the same vicinity. This would include a home office if distributing on a small scale, or a large warehouse if making plans to distribute nationally.

For more information about the laws in your state, please visit https://www.ttb.gov/importers/importer_regs.shtml

Getting Started with Wine Imports

Wine and spirits makers are enthusiastic about their art and the nature of their products. They take incredible considerations to guarantee that their yield satisfies their high standards.

You are likewise worried about the wine's appropriation: guaranteeing that the item that leaves their facility is transported securely and is undiminished in quality when it arrives in the glasses of your clients.

In pondering the wine and spirits industry, we will spotlight those two bookend segments: the creation and the client experience.

Significant work happens in the middle of this process - from the coordination of packaging, bundling, putting away, transporting, and conveying the items.

Because enormous advances in these areas are made every day, it may be ideal to consider your current procedures and the manners by which they can be streamlined.

The following are 10 thoughts to enable an organization to streamline its wine coordination activity.

Infrastructure

As a wine importer or wholesaler, you will often be faced with massive amounts of paperwork.

Unlike other industries in the market, the importing and distribution of wine requires every piece of documentation needed for importing goods and products into the U.S. It also requires tax reporting.

There are plenty of software applications on the market available to help you manage this paperwork. These software packages are designed exclusively for wine importers and wholesalers.

Let's look at the top benefits of having an import enterprise software in your arsenal.

But first, we will discuss what you need to track for your business and what any software you choose should manage for you.

Landed Cost Evaluation

The "landed cost" feature is one that collects data from all of the total transactions completed over a certain period of time.

Typically, it consists of the first two fiscal quarters of data. This data provides the landed cost, on average, and calculates the cost at the individual shipment level in real time, while the goods are being transported.

The base cost is the original purchase price of the goods, with the option of adding more traditional costs like freight fees and insurance costs.

You can obtain these figures from the invoices you will get with your shipments. With this type of feature, you can rely more on real-time data, vs. average costs of the industry.

This puts you at an advantage of knowing exactly what the price your customers need to pay for your wine in order for you to make a profit.

Profitability

Enterprise software for importers has a feature that enables you to keep track of your inventory match specific wines with customer orders.

Whether you choose to do this manually or automatically, the software is intuitive enough to know what the inventory and the projected cost is. It will add it to the current sales order, giving you instant access to the profitability of each sale, simply with the click of your mouse.

Future Planning

Inventory visibility is often a great challenge for customers who do not keep boxes and crates of wines in their home office where they can physically see them.

One of the reporting features of enterprise software for importers is the feature that shows you everything you currently have in your supply chain. It is typically reported in a spreadsheet form of some sort, depending on the software you choose.

You will have the option of seeing where your inventory is at all times, whether it is in transit or sitting in a warehouse.

You can also determine which wines are going to be shipped directly to your customers. You can apply the appropriate sales order number and information to that shipment, so you always know what you have sold and what you need to re-order.

Share More Efficiently

As a wine importer, you are constantly moving about. The ability to communicate with back-office documents, applications, and organizations is even more critical.

Whether you decide to go with a cloud version or desktop version of a software, you have the ability to set up access for your team with merely a computer and internet connection.

Your sales team, for example, will always have real-time data on what they need to focus on selling. It can even help you manage customer queries without having to speak to anyone over the phone.

If you plan to travel yourself to get wine, you may be out of touch. But with enterprise software, you can set up access for your vendors and customers alike. You will always be in the loop, as well as with anyone else you wish to have access.

Document Processing and Preparation

Enterprise software for importers allows you to manage all of your pre-order processing functions. You can complete work inquiries, fulfill quotes, and more.

Each function will be tracked in the system and can be assigned to an individual member of your team for follow up on a date of your choosing.

This is a great way to keep everything on track, so deadlines aren't missed. You can even add your consultants and stay up to date with application and renewal deadlines.

Most of the software available is integrated with Microsoft, where you can generate sales and purchase orders, customer invoices, and various other documents using Word or Excel.

You can also automatically generate the specific forms required by the government agencies like the Customs and Border Protection agency.

Some Software Suggestions

One of the top companies that I have the most experience within this area is called VISCO (http://viscosoftware.com/)

You can obtain this software for a mere $19.99 per year. VISCO can keep your wine import business on track and organized.

Another import and export software is called BlueLink (https://www.bluelinkerp.com/import-export-inventory-accounting-software/).

Blue Link has been designed from the ground up for wholesalers and distributors and contains several of the features that are important for success in this business.

Logistics

If you are one of those people who like to outsource to save time, then this next section will appeal more to you.

Here we will go into the details of how to hire companies to do all the backend functions for you. This means you don't have to have the software and infrastructures in place, they already do and do it quite well.

That would mean you would have to give up some of your profit in order to pay them for their services. This is a great way to get started without any personal risk.

Having your wine stored in a TTB-bonded warehouse is extremely beneficial for new wine importers, especially when you take into consideration the aspects involved around safety, security, storage space, and proper storage conditions.

While saving you tons of money on the storage space, you won't have to pay any excise taxes on the stored product in bond. You will only be required to pay taxes when the product has left the warehouse and has been shipped to you or your customers.

Shipping & Bottling

We, in the importing world, have a love/hate relationship with glass.

It's pretty and serves as an effective container, but glass is likewise delicate, which adds to your transportation costs.

By shipping your wine in spacious compartments and waiting out the packaging to the end, you can decrease shipment costs, improve the timeframe of realistic usability, and dispose of the risks of glass being harmed in travel.

In particular, enhancements have guaranteed that the quality and trustworthiness of your items won't be undermined during shipment.

Analysis of mass imports of wine by the Waste Resources Action Program demonstrates that temperature soundness is "improved by mass shipment since a bigger single volume of fluid has more prominent warm dormancy than a smaller one."

You can additionally diminish costs and improve process duration by transporting your mass fluids to an outsider coordinator's supplier who can supply the whole process of packaging, bundling, stockpiling, and conveyance under one roof.

Consider Transportation Options

On-the-road transportation can cost about $5,000 per trailer cross-country.

As each rail vehicle holds around three trailers of merchandise, you can decrease transportation expenses and your carbon footprint by utilizing rail transportation as a major aspect of your system.

In its Green Freight Handbook, the Environmental Defense Fund gauges that you can diminish fuel costs by 16 -21% by changing from truck to rail.

Every part of rail shipping has been streamlined to be more efficient than any other time in recent memory.

Gone are the times of different contracts with numerous railyards and various merchants. All transactions for railway use can be completed by one entity.

Cross-Docking

Get them in and get them out!

Cross-docking is the approach of sending an impending shipment of wine from a truck, trailer, or rail vehicle out for distribution right away.

That is, the products land on the dock and go directly out for dispersion, with no need for storage.

Government law expresses that, for a shipper to dispatch Direct-To-Consumer (DTC), they should meet two prerequisites:

1. The merchant needs a Federal Basic Permit to import wine.
2. They should conform to all state and nearby laws for the states to which they need to deliver.

Numerous states such as those listed here require an immediate transportation grant, a permit expense, an application charge, deals and extract duties, and detailing.

- Louisiana
- Nebraska
- New Hampshire
- Nevada
- North Dakota
- Oregon
- Virginia
- Wyoming
- West Virginia

Most states will limit the kinds of organizations that can obtain a grant for DTC deals.

Contact data, including sites for the liquor refreshment control board in each state, can be found on the Wine Institute site.

Logistic Partner Capacity

On the off chance that you have a great deal of stock at a factory, you have a ton of stock that's housed far from your clients.

Consider joining forces with a coordination organization, known as a logistics provider, with the ability to deal with all the business you can give it.

A powerful 3PL (third-party logistics) supplier can appropriate your stock flawlessly. They can guarantee that there are no bottlenecks in the outbound production network, no demurrage charges, squandered travel costs, and no interruptions amid low or intense interest periods.

Distribute Regionally

Having one storage facility for your entire inventory may not be ideal.

Regional distribution centers have the ability to reduce costs by reducing the distance shipments must travel to the final wholesaler.

While additional facilities do come with additional space and inventory costs, transportation costs are the largest drain on your bottom line.

In terms of demand, regional distribution centers allow you to fulfill orders and efficiently meet the demands of your wholesale customers.

Finally, regional distribution allows you to spread the risk of damage to your inventory across multiple locations in the event of a disaster or other major disruption.

Share Your Loads

Collaboration in logistics is rare among wine and spirits competitors. For that reason, you might find two half-filled trucks from the same region pulled up, side-by-side, at the exact same wholesale distribution center.

How crazy is that? It's like taking a cab to the airport and running into your neighbor, who booked and paid for his own cab.

For maximum freight efficiency, it helps to think "We," not "Me." Consolidating loads with nearby competitors could cut your LTL (life-to-load) costs as much as 25%.

As an example, Kane works with a mid-sized consumer packaged goods (CPG) manufacturer who was spending $632,000 annually on LTL shipments.

After introducing consolidation into the equation, Kane reduced the cost for the same volume of freight to $467,680. That's a savings of $164,320.

It may be time for wine and spirits manufacturers to innovate in this area.

All of these critical areas of logistics can be handled by an outside company. Consider which one provides everything you need, do diligent research on them, check reviews, and confirm their bond status.

How to Private Label Your Wine Import Business

The private label wine business is increasing as retailers and eateries search for approaches to create a one-of-a-kind brand identity.

Why Create a Private Label

Private labeled wines are turning into an undeniably popular portion of the U.S. wine industry. Propelling your own private labeled wine can increase your income and help you make an exceptional brand personality that separates you from the competition

Maybe the best case of a private label wine business taking off is the Kirkland Signature line of wines at Costco. Costco is currently the top wine retailer in the U.S.

Through its elite associations with wineries in the United States, Costco can offer interesting, premium wines at a large portion of the expense of anyplace else.

Likewise, companies like Trader Joe's have sold more than 50 million cases of its own private label wine dating back to 2002.

Similarly, a rising number of stores, including some of the national and domestic wine brands and liquor store chains, are following in their footsteps. They are taking on the private label wine import business as a sure-fire way to increase their bottom line and grow their profit margins significantly.

According to some studies, the profit margins available when private labeling your wine is anywhere from 12-16% higher than on those directly available from national brands like Whitetail or Barefoot.

Current market research indicates that private labeled wines account for more than 5% of all of the total wine sales in the US. In the next few years, that figure will be much higher.

Some of the projections available estimate it to be at about 20% of the entire wine market in coming years.

That would essentially put the private label wine industry at the equivalent of other private labeled goods.

In the French and Italian markets, private labeled wines are more popular. They account for more than 1/3 of the total wine sales in the region.

Not only does private labeling your wine have an economic appeal, but the brand identity can also help you stand out in restaurants, hotels, and retailers across the country.

For instance, the incredible Italian eatery Carmine's in New York City has utilized private mark wines as a major aspect of its general marketing technique.

The significant point to remember is that a private label wine doesn't state "private name" on the container. To the casual wine consumer, it looks simply like some other wine they may drink.

While Costco and Trader Joe's clients may understand they are drinking private label wines, that assumption is not really valid in the café and hospitality business.

Having an eye-catching name is just as compelling as having a top of the line wine.

All things considered, the container, the stopper, and the name are the same.

It's simply a question of persuading a client to attempt a $10-15 bottle of wine they may not have tried before rather than a jug of wine they are familiar with that is 2-3 times as costly.

How Do You Begin

First, determine the type of wine that your customers are consuming and what price they are paying for these bottles. From there, you can then make effective projections about the stability and growth of your wine imports and the business as a whole.

Don't order hundreds or thousands of cases of wine at a time that no one wants, just to be stuck with inventory you cannot move.

The wines that you ultimately choose must be a natural choice for the buyer, according to the region and style of the wine they serve to their customers.

Reach out to the various wineries in the area that could potentially be of interest in making a deal with you.

With your narrowed down list of options, from there you can expect the vintner to work with you as the importer on every single detail of how your wine is created and packaged and even as specific as the type of cork you prefer to use.

Look for design companies to help you design your label, your cases, and the promotional materials you need to market your wine portfolio.

The label they create will need to meet the standards and specifications required of the country you wish to sell your wine.

From that point, all you need to do is to place an order. You will be on your way to having your own wine importing business without putting in much capital.

Once you have decided on the right private label company, work on defining the countries you wish to work in.

In the next section, we will discuss how to go about finding these countries and what to look for when deciding to import wine from them.

How to Find Good Wineries

When I began focusing on who was bringing in my preferred wines, I saw a theme of similar names.

I adore high corrosive, light-bodied, low-mediation wines. Discovering shippers like Selection Massale and Percy Selections, who have some expertise in those sorts of wines, completely changed my wine drinking habits.

Every merchant has their favored styles of wines that they appreciate, regardless of whether it be French wines, blockbuster reds, or common wines.

In case you see similar names spring up, you know their favored style of wine is your style as well.

We're instructed to search for wine by varietals we like or by areas we know. This is certainly not an awful way to do it, yet it overlooks the impact of the maker.

Whatever the grapes might be, and wherever they might be developed, it truly comes down to what the winemaker chooses to do with them.

This is the reason snatching any Sangiovese from Tuscany off the rack doesn't promise it will be in a similar style as that Sangiovese from Tuscany at that Italian Spot in Chicago you adored.

Shopping by the merchant, you know and trust the shipper. With that being stated, not all shippers are made the same.

Keep notes on wines you like. Converse with sommeliers and storekeepers about what you like in wine. Check whether they have any merchants they would recommend.

Shopping by the merchant is one of the main approaches to finding low-mediation wines. These wines are made with natural grapes, no synthetic concoctions, and usually, contain a negligible amount of sulfites.

Shopping along these lines gives you a chance to investigate wines that maybe you wouldn't really take a second look at. It is very simple to fall into the comfort of drinking what sorts of wine we know from regions we're comfortable with.

Focus on the countries who have the wine that you want and let your private label company know if that's what you choose to do to get started.

Once you know where you are going to get your product, it's time to learn where to get your buyers.

How to Find Your Target Market

Your success in the wine importing business will hinge upon your knowledge of who your low-hanging fruit, or ideal target market, may be.

As the wine import industry explodes, being able to maintain your competitive advantage is becoming more difficult to achieve.

ving great tasting wine is merely not
, although it is the foundation for creating a
w.. mport business.

You also have to know who you are leaving a mark on and who is drinking your wine on a consistent basis.

I'm going to show you the significance of knowing who these customers are, how to go about finding who they are, and what you must do once you gain that knowledge.

The Who

Let's start with the obvious question: Who is your ideal target market?

Before you can start planning an event, or creating any promotional materials, you must define who you are targeting.

Many wine importers make the mistake of not being specific enough in their targeting.

For example, a pizza place will say it targets anyone who eats pizza.

The reality of the situation is that not all pizza consumers are the same.

There are younger millennials who want to use a mobile app and have their favorite chicken BBQ pizza available to order at their fingertips.

There are elderly couples who are looking for a thin-crust, meat lover's pizza to eat with a glass of wine on their terrace.

Having a broad and ambiguous audience makes it challenging for you to pinpoint who your true customers are, and therefore deliver to them what they seek.

Please don't go into your wine importing business targeting everyone who drinks wine. That's not the right way to go about it.

Who is drinking your wine? Why are they drinking your wine, and what brands do they prefer?

Start by further refining who they are by using the most common types of demographics, and then ask yourself more specific types of questions.

Eventually, you will have gathered enough information to take the generalities and make them specific and tangible characteristics that you can market to.

The What

Keep these questions in mind when you are brainstorming and doing your evaluation.

- How old are the people drinking your wine?
- What are their age brackets?
- Are there more women than men buyers?
- Do your customers shop for wine as a family or with friends?
- Does your customer have a certain type of fashion sense?
- Do your customers use social media?
- Are they tech savvy?
- What days are the most wines shipped and sold? Why?

- Do you often get asked about food pairing with your wines?
- Do your customers have household pets?

These sample questions will reveal a great bit of information about who your ideal target market is and should inspire you to dive deeper into their motivations, desires, and buying behaviors.

You will soon discover who your true and loyal customers are.

The Where

To learn the most information about your customers, you can do surveys, hold online meetings via video conferencing, or teach a wine tip each week.

Ask industry experts. You can question the wine attendant in a restaurant to a seasoned sommelier. Each of these people has a different relationship and ultimately, interaction with the wine buyers you wish to target.

They each bring differing perspectives to light, which can help you deliver a richly satisfying experience to your customers.

The How

The key is to take the information and actually deliver on what you found, and what your customers want.

Do not be surprised if you have more than one type of ideal customer.

Once you have identified who they are, you can then begin to roll-out initiatives that will speak to each one of them. This will make them loyal to your brand and repeat returning customers.

Knowing your customers shows you how to appeal to them and their demands and interests.

If you determine that your target happens to be women from the ages of 21 to 35, start by focusing on social media. In particular, Instagram is heavily populated with this demographic.

Once you have your Instagram account aesthetically pleasing to your customers, and you have gained a significant following, you can then use it to promote any wine-tastings or events you may have.

Specifically use it to showcase the release of new wine into your inventory, or a wine of the month club with a food pairing tip.

If nothing else, use it to let people know of discounts, specials, and holiday bundles you are offering.

If your target is men and women who are between the ages of 34-55, you will want to collect their email addresses and start building your marketing list.

This particular age group always checks their emails. They mostly rely on the information they receive from outside sources. This means that you can message them once a month with a newsletter including all of your promotions, specials, and wine clubs.

Understanding and knowing without a doubt who your customers are will give you new and exciting ways of keeping your customer satisfied.

Remain attentive to what your customers' needs are and be sure to deliver what they are asking for in new and creative ways. This will keep you at a competitive advantage in the ever increasing market.

How will you connect with your market? Will you sell on the web? Simply setting up an online store isn't sufficient to drive traffic and fill shopping baskets.

On the off chance that you have a tasting room, you have that as a driver for future online purchases

On the off chance that you don't, you should discover different approaches to direct people to your site and to advertise wine club memberships.

In the next chapter, we will discuss profit and growth within the wine import industry and how you can maintain a lucrative and sustainable business.

Profit and Growth

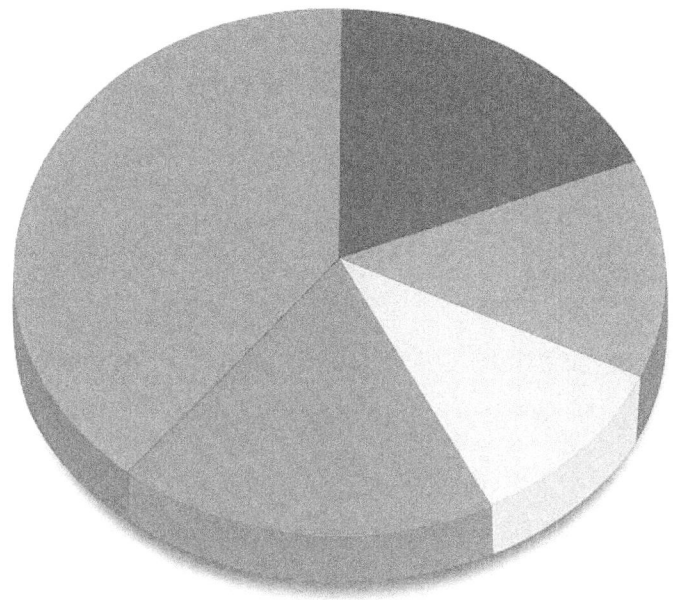

Pricing your wine for profit and exposure can be difficult.

Despite what type of knowledge customers have about wine, many wine consumers select their wine first based on the type of wine it is then, secondly the price of the wine.

The wine buyer will first go to the section of wine they enjoy most, whether it is white or red, for example, and then on to the specific types of wine within each, for example, a mild merlot in the red, or a Pinot in the white.

After they have found their flavor and type, they will go with the best price.

Typically, this process automatically limits the customer's selection. There will still be a large number of variations to choose from, which can often be discouraging to new wine enthusiasts.

It's your job to help the process become easier for them.

I'll share with you a few pricing models and guidelines to help you get started learning how to price the wines you have decided to purchase.

It's not just about profit, but also for exposure in order to grow your portfolio. I'll show you the pathway for setting yourself up for success as you acquire more wines.

Eventually, as you grow your wine portfolio, you will want to consider expanding into other regions of the country and the globe.

Specific wines are rare in some areas, and you could do well to be their exclusive connection to obtaining it at a reasonable price.

We'll go over the best ways to grow your portfolio. In the next chapter, we will discuss the details of expanding across multiple states.

Despite what you might think, there is a lot of thought that goes into a bottle of wine and at what price to sell it for. There are several different pricing systems in the wine industry that include terms like, "ultra-premium," or "popular premium," you might have even heard of "super value."

How much should you anticipate spending on a decent bottle of wine? After doing research on wine prices, segmentation, and observing major retail stores online, I've been able to come to a tentative analysis that on average, a bottle runs about $20 in the U.S.

Understanding Cash Flow

The statement of income indicates how an organization spends its cash (money outflow) and from where an organization gets its cash (money inflow).

The cash flow proclamation incorporates all money an organization takes in.

In this section of the chapter, we'll clarify the income cash flow statement and how it can enable you to dissect an organization's investment ability.

There are two types of bookkeeping - money and accumulation. This is also referred to as cash and accrual

Accumulation bookkeeping is the bookkeeping technique where income is accounted for as pay when it's earned as opposed to when the organization gets installment. Costs are accounted for when brought about despite the fact that no money installments have been made.

For instance, if an organization records a deal, the income is perceived on the pay proclamation. However, the organization may not get the money until a later date.

The deal would be recorded as receivable with no effect on actual money until the invoice was remitted.

Pricing

When it comes to increasing wine sales, it is important to consider the "contribution margin," while also adding to your profit margin levels.

If you apply a standard percentage of margin, you are not doing yourself any favors in the long run. It's a poor way to increase wine sales.

Cost of goods sold is never really a good indication of the actual profit. That's when you need to take a look at the calculations of the contributing margin.

No wine importer is going to object to selling more wine. Neither is any retailer or venue.

It's ultimately the goal of any wine importing business to make money and sell wine, while steadily increasing the bottom line.

As your business grows, it's only natural that your wine sales will increase, just like they would automatically increase if you have a sale or an exclusive bottle of wine available.

Discounting the price or dropping prices for a specific period of time will have a more negative impact on your profits than positive.

You will constantly be looking for ways to make up for the losses and offering to drop prices lower is the natural and first instinct. That doesn't necessarily mean more money. It means less inventory.

Understanding COGS

The term "cost of goods sold" or "COGS" is figured at the beginning of the inventory costs accrued, any extra inventory costs that may come up, minus your ending inventory, which is equal to the COGS during a financial, fiscal year.

This may be a bit confusing, but let's break it down with a real-world example.

Let's say you buy a bottle of wine overseas for $20, and sell it for $60.00. That's essentially a 300% mark-up that generates a 33 percent COGS rate.

Easy when you put it that way, right?

CFOs and business owners across the country use this calculation in all types of business models. Have an established back-end capable of supporting monitoring your COGS. We examined software choices in a previous chapter.

If you have a better understanding of the definitive relationship with cost, volume, and profit margin, it will lead to having potentially larger profits.

It's helpful to know this when you want to focus on being a wholesaler and distributor. There are times when dealing with retailers where this will come up a lot, and you want to be able to answer their tough and thorough questions.

Please know, there are many more factors at play that will determine at what price point you can sell your wine without losing money.

Putting together a series of different prices and sales stats will help you to make an argument for using contribution margin as the sole means of generating higher profits.

Growing Your Wine Portfolio

Here are a few tips on how you get your wine from your generation line onto the racks of retailers and into the beverage menu of eateries.

Buy Low

You ought to purchase hard and low.

Each penny saved on your cost will be used somewhere else. Shippers, merchants, and retailers will add to your costs.

Try not to hold back on quality. Attempt to get the ideal arrangement for your dollar.

Have One Line Price

Have a set line cost and rundown all marks in the line at your value point.

Basic sells.

Marketing is about observation, so let the brand send a consistent message.

When you set one cost for your line, it's simple for your wholesaler, your retailer, and your customers to remember your product. Regardless of whether you will lose a little on one of your names, it's smarter to keep up your image at that point.

Profit Margin

Plan on 40% margin for your distributor.

Permitting your merchants a possibility of a 40% margin gives them the motivating force they have to put your image at the highest point of their needs list.

The more overall revenue you can offer them, the more lured they will be to enable you to move your cases.

Have a Marketing Budget

Consider spending much on your brand's website. Making a good impression online is key.

How will you gain new clients?

Aside from the marketing considerations discussed in a previous chapter, these new clients are obtained both by online means (social media, website) and also through utilizing a tasting room.

Running a physical location where clients can sample your wines leads to several advantages.

- They create a specific setting surrounding your wine and your image.
- They give a chance to agree to accept a wine club membership directly where clients are generally locked in.

- Positive sentiments made amid the personal experience can drive future sales on the website and further wine club deals.

In this manner, tasting rooms frequently convey their weight with regards to showcasing your items.

Tasting rooms have their very own arrangement of difficulties. One consideration is the very administration of running a physical location for tasting your products.

Put some genuine idea into the earning potential of the original investment point for your tasting room. Do some exploration to discover what the guidelines are for tasting rooms in your state.

Warehousing Costs to Consider

Warehousing and satisfaction are frequently observed as two separate sides of a similar coin. You can draw in an accomplice for taking care of one, the other, or both.

Normally a satisfaction focus doesn't mean a reinforced office. The satisfaction focus would just need enough duty paid stock available to take care of a specific measure of requests.

For instance, they may just need a 30 or multi-day supply of the SKUs you are selling. When that stock is exhausted, the winery will make good on any regulatory expenses to the administration, and afterward, the item will move from the reinforced storeroom to a satisfaction task.

Therefore, numerous wineries will utilize a long haul stockpiling stockroom to store most of their merchandise until the time has come to sell the item.

As long as shippers make good on their government obligation at the time of import and retailers make good on regulatory obligation at the season of procurement from a winery or merchant, the stock is in fact charge paid. The stock can go legitimately to a satisfaction focus when required or else remain in a long haul storeroom.

Expanding to Multiple States

Working an effective, streamlined wine business across state lines is fantastically convoluted.

Alcohol laws differ from state to state.

Therefore, wine executives must work with individual providers and wholesalers in each state, muddling their occupations massively.

Research New Markets

At Barteca, which has a chain of 29 cafés, wine and spirits executive Gretchen Thomas has her hands full. She is preparing to open 11 new eateries across the nation.

Barteca can be found in around twelve states along the East Coast, including New York, Virginia, and Florida. It likewise has cafés as far west as Colorado.

With 150 providers for Barteca's Barcelona Wine Bar's refreshment program alone, which can incorporate up to 400 wines, Thomas says she utilizes a mammoth spreadsheet.

She begins reaching every provider around four months before opening in another market to discover who may work in that specific state and which wines are accessible.

The objective, she says, is to open new cafés with comparable records, so the servers and their coaches who fly in from different urban areas are now acquainted with the wines on opening day.

Thomas clarifies that another eatery can regularly work as a representative for opening new markets for Spanish wines.

Particularly while going into another market, understanding that state's laws and guidelines can be testing.

State laws can likewise considerably influence the costs and accessibility of items offered to purchasers.

Thomas found out about this when Barteca first opened its eateries in Virginia three years prior. While wine is offered through merchants in the state, alcohol is constrained by a state-run element.

Thomas began making mixed drinks with sherry, vermouth, and port wine since those fixings were promptly accessible from wine merchants.

State Restrictions

Most states have statutory arrangements that take into consideration out-of-state producers. Most states confine immediate shipments to wine.

Out of 54 states, domains, and regions, of the US, three states—Alabama, Oklahoma, and Utah—explicitly restrict the immediate shipment of mixed refreshments to buyers.

Mississippi, Guam, Puerto Rico, and the U.S. Virgin Islands don't have rules that determine which immediate shipments are permitted.

Massachusetts and Pennsylvania have had resolutions ruled illegal by state courts in those states.

Delaware has statutory arrangements that expect requests to be prepared and dispatched through authorized wholesalers.

Arizona, Arkansas, Georgia, Kentucky, and South Carolina have statutory arrangements that enable the wine to be delivered to the state when acquired by the client on location at the winery.

Rhode Island enables inebriating drinks to be sent when acquired nearby.

Five states - Arizona, Florida, Hawaii, Nebraska, and New Hampshire, and the District of Columbia - approve the immediate shipment of all spirits as indicated.

Eight states permit the immediate shipment of lager and wine as determined:

- Delaware
- Massachusetts
- Montana
- North Dakota
- Ohio
- Oregon
- Vermont
- Virginia

The rest of the states only permit direct wine shipments.

Standing Out From the Crowd

As we kick off the chapter, I'll teach you how to avoid burning out before your flame is fully lit.

It is a competitive economy. Merely doing the minimum is not nearly enough to keep you ahead of the pack.

Understanding how to stay fresh and build your brand is imperative.

These components are not one and the same, but one cannot be done without nurturing the other.

I'll show you how to do both, as well as how to use social media to your best advantage and become a social media ninja.

Last and most certainly not least, we will talk about educating yourself and your customers and how you interact with them to wow them with each experience with your business.

It's one thing to be great at what you do. You can be the best and still not be perceived.

Know Yourself

This may appear glaringly evident, yet individuals are vague on their preferences and their identity as an individual.

This is particularly valid for the more those of a more established age; we were not given the elbow room to investigate and communicate, and we didn't have the instrument of the web to do this.

We were urged to resemble every other person and fit in perfectly with society.

I know when I was more youthful, I didn't know what I preferred, considering that I hadn't investigated life enough to know myself.

Having mindfulness builds up your identity. Your demeanor to the world will mirror your loves and interests.

Investigate the world, regardless of how old you are, whether you trust you know yourself or not.

Have a go at something you've been itching to do. Propelling yourself outside your usual range of familiarity will push you towards realizing yourself better.

To have a powerful urge toward something is the importance of life. You adore doing it; you lose all sense of direction in it, you forget about time.

Your energy lies in getting the hang of, making, and exceeding expectations in whatever it is that interests you.

You cannot have the energy for something you fiddle with sporadically and apathetically.

To be energetic about something is to need to partake in it constantly. You need to find out about it. You may even be a little fixated on it.

Make it a colossal piece of your life. Take the plunge!

In the event that you adore something, plunge into it. Devour it.

Has it turned into a piece of your identity? Make it your lifestyle. This is the thing that builds up your uniqueness and makes you great in what you want to do.

Surviving Start-Up Burn Out

There are numerous daily deadlines, urgent tasks to deal with, and fires to put out.

Not to mention the competitiveness of the wine import business can leave you feeling a bit overwhelmed at first. You can run the risk of burn-out.

I'm going to share the experience I have often felt during my career to help you avoid it altogether and remain a thriving wine importer and entrepreneur.

Watch out for the warning signs. Burn-out doesn't happen overnight.

It builds up slowly and over time and will not always present itself outright. When it does, it will slip into not only your work life but your social life too.

If you have a habit of pleasing everyone, by over-committing yourself and making too many promises, you are more susceptible to burn-out.

If you find your body giving you warning signs, please take heed.

You'll notice that you feel tired all of the time, grouchy, irritable, and in extreme cases, you can experience disabling fatigue and insomnia.

It is important you recognize these warning signs early on and act on them.

Take a step back. Take a couple of days off. Say no when you can.

Try not to work crazy hours or inconsistent shifts, even from your home office. It's easier not to get up and go have time for yourself when your office is right in your home.

Ask questions about other areas of your life as well. Constantly ask yourself what you can do today to make your life easier and more in control of tomorrow.

You can't work on building your brand and staying fresh in the industry if you are constantly burn-out.

Building a Brand

Setting yourself apart from your competitors is a primary challenge for wine importers of all stages of their business.

What does it take for a customer to say yes to a wine?

How do you attract customers to your brand when they have never even heard of you or tasted your wine?

Those are good questions to ask yourself when deciding how to stay fresh, but is that helping you build your brand?

Branding is a big buzzword in the wine industry. From restaurants to hotels, businesses are focusing more on their branding strategies.

Are you a fad? Are you a brand that will be around for a long time?

For wine importers, branding is the process of being able to identify the central characteristics of the business, what it stands for and against, and how you want the public to perceive you.

Then it's about taking that knowledge and delivering the wines, products, and services that bring those characteristics you identified to live.

Put more simply, branding, as it relates here, is the very essence of a business defined in clearly tangible ways.

Today's wine buyers have more demands and wants, and fewer hours to entertain themselves in.

A business that has a clearly established brand can build relationships with its customers.

This is done through emotional connections and the satisfaction of basic human needs.

The bottom line is that a brand is a business promise, from you to your customers.

It sets expectations between the two of you without any words and without a formal written contract.

Think of it as an unwritten warranty on a car. It's a symbol of integrity, and more importantly, it's a reputation.

Be sure you aren't confusing your brand with your product, which is the actual wine that is for sale.

Your wine becomes more valuable when you attach it to a clearly recognizable name brand and a clear promise of your intentions and authenticity.

Building a unique brand for your wine importing business will take a little bit of your imagination, some patience, and discipline, and even collaboration with outside resources to actually get it all implemented.

Your business' "identity" - or marking - should separate you from different bottles on the rack.

On an equivalent value playing field, clients might be pulled into bottles that mirror their own identities; a clever or harsh name and logo, for example, may entice a client who shares that identity over a plainer, increasingly refined marking that may draw in an alternate customer.

Your wine jug's shading, logo, and mark, including your wine depiction, impact a client's choice to purchase your wine.

Referrals from Customers

Wine is typically shared, which impacts consumer loyalty, dedication, and new client enrollment.

In the event that your wine is chosen for an evening gathering, for example, the hostess has likely incorporated your wine because she appreciates it.

She has confidence that her visitors will also.

Provided that this is true, her guests may purchase your wine on their own based on her recommendation and join your group of faithful clients.

Suggestions and insistences from individual customers and wine shop staff are regularly made, too.

Social media comments are the direct line to consumer's comments, thoughts, and suggestions. You may also want to consider soliciting reviews on your website and then incorporating those testimonials in your marketing campaigns.

Customer Loyalty

Choosing a most loved wine brand can be a long procedure. If clients enjoy one type of your line, they are likely to purchase your wine again, and even branch out into other wine types from your selection.

One of the greatest difficulties that businesses face is the disparities between various ages' purchasing behaviors.

Baby boomers, for example, are scaling down and needless decisions. With regards to wine brands, the greater part doesn't offer the consistency of advertising and brand message that this demographic responds to.

Educate Your Customers

There is an overflow of information on the internet about wines, but not an equal amount of information on how to get started educating yourself or what to begin with first.

Understanding and learning about wine is not everyone's cup of tea.

If you plan on being successful as a wine importer, this education is imperative. Direct interaction with wine is the best way for wine drinkers and importers to increase their experiences and gain an improved pallet.

The first thing you must do is change the way you drink wine. The ultimate goal is not to help you drink more, but to change the way you currently buy wine and ultimately consume it.

You are not just a wine consumer; you are in the business of selling it, and you need to know what you are selling.

Learn about the styles of wine available. What kinds of wine exist around the world?

Even though there are literally thousands of wines produced and manufactured each year, all with a distinct taste, there are only 9 underlying styles that ultimately define the wine market scope.

You will want to taste from each one of the different styles so you can understand the range involved in wine.

Once you know and are familiar with the tastes of the 9 styles of wine, then it's time to move on to learn the two critical and basic wine standards of etiquette - how the wine is tasted and how the wine is preserved.

Nothing else is important here. Every winemaker will attest to this.

Once you have educated yourself, it's much easier to answer your customers' questions. Nobody wants to purchase a product or service, especially something as personal as wine, from someone who does not know anything about what they are selling.

I've provided you with some bonus material. In the Glossary, you can find wine shipping laws for each of the 50 states so you can decide where you want to establish your business and where you want to establish yourself as a foreign entity doing business.

Glossary of Wine Shipping Laws by State

Source: United States Customs Enforcement

Alabama

Direct shipping is prohibited. Consumers may order wines from out-of-state wineries, but must obtain permission from the state liquor authority and have the wine sent to an ABC store for pickup and payment of taxes.

Alaska

Winery direct shipping permitted; direct retailer shipping permitted, except to dry communities.

Arizona

Winery direct shipping permitted. Retailer shipping prohibited.

Arkansas

Direct shipping prohibited, with an on-site exception. Consumers must visit the winery in person to have wine shipped to their home, up to 1 case per calendar quarter. Retailer shipping prohibited.

California

Winery direct shipping permitted; reciprocal retailer shipping permitted.

Colorado

Winery direct shipping permitted; retailer shipping prohibited.

Connecticut

Winery direct shipping permitted, up to 5 gallons every two months; retailer shipping prohibited.

Delaware

Direct shipping prohibited, with on-site exception: Delaware residents may visit an out-of-state winery and bring or ship wine back to their homes, but shipping by common carriers (FedEx, UPS) is prohibited. Retailer shipping prohibited.

District of Columbia

Winery direct shipping permitted, up to 1 case per month; retailer shipping permitted.

Florida

Winery direct shipping permitted; retailer shipping prohibited.

Georgia

Winery direct shipping permitted, up to 12 cases per year; retailer shipping prohibited.

Hawaii

Winery direct shipping permitted, up to 6 cases per year; retailer shipping prohibited.

Idaho

Winery direct shipping permitted, up to 24 cases per year; retailer shipping prohibited.

Illinois

Winery direct shipping permitted, up to 12 cases per year; retailer shipping prohibited.

Indiana

Winery direct shipping permitted, up to 24 cases per year; retailer shipping prohibited.

Iowa

Winery direct shipping permitted; retailer shipping prohibited.

Kansas

Winery direct shipping permitted, up to 12 cases per year; retailer shipping prohibited.

Kentucky

Prohibitively limited winery direct shipping. Kentucky residents may have wine shipped to them from small wineries making 50,000 gallons of wine or less per year, except in dry counties; however, common carriers (FedEx, UPS) will not deliver to Kentucky. Retailer shipping prohibited.

Louisiana

Limited winery direct shipping permitted. Wineries may ship wines that are not carried by a Louisiana distributor, up to 12 cases per year. Retailer shipping permitted.

Maine

Winery direct shipping permitted, up to 12 cases per year; retailer shipping prohibited.

Maryland

Winery direct shipping permitted, up to 18 cases per year; retailer shipping prohibited.

Massachusetts

Winery direct shipping permitted, effective Jan. 1, 2015, up to 12 cases per year; retailer shipping prohibited.

Michigan

Winery direct shipping permitted; retailer shipping prohibited.

Minnesota

Winery direct shipping permitted, up to 2 cases per year; retailer shipping prohibited.

Mississippi

Direct shipping prohibited.

Missouri

Winery direct shipping permitted, up to 2 cases per month; retailer direct shipping prohibited.

Montana

Winery direct shipping permitted, up to 18 cases per year; retailer direct shipping prohibited.

Nebraska

Winery direct shipping permitted, up to 1 case per month; retailer shipping permitted.

Nevada

Winery direct shipping permitted, up to 12 cases per year; retailer shipping permitted.

New Hampshire

Winery direct shipping permitted, up to 12 cases per year; retailer shipping permitted.

New Jersey

Limited winery direct shipping. New Jersey residents may have up to 12 cases of wine per year shipped to their home from small wineries making 250,000 gallons of wine or less per year. Retailer shipping prohibited.

New Mexico

Winery direct shipping permitted, up to 2 cases per month; reciprocal retailer shipping permitted.

New York

Winery direct shipping permitted, up to 36 cases per year; retailer shipping prohibited.

North Carolina

Winery direct shipping permitted, up to 2 cases per month; retailer shipping prohibited.

North Dakota

Winery direct shipping permitted; retailer shipping permitted.

Ohio

Limited winery direct shipping. Ohio residents may have up to 24 cases of wine per year shipped to their home from small wineries making 250,000 gallons of wine or less per year. Retailer shipping prohibited.

Oklahoma

Winery direct shipping permitted, effective October 2018.

Oregon

Winery direct shipping permitted, up to 2 cases per month; retailer shipping permitted.

Pennsylvania

Winery direct shipping permitted, up to 36 cases per year; retailer shipping prohibited.

Rhode Island

Direct shipping prohibited, with an on-site exception. Rhode Island residents may visit an out-of-state winery and have wine shipped to them; however, it is illegal for a common carrier (FedEx, UPS) to deliver wine in Rhode Island to anyone who does not have a valid wholesaler license. Retailer shipping prohibited.

South Carolina

Winery direct shipping permitted, up to 2 cases per month; retailer shipping prohibited.

South Dakota

Effective January 2016, direct winery shipping permitted, up to 12 cases per year; retailer shipping prohibited.

Tennessee

Winery direct shipping permitted, up to 3 cases per year; retailer shipping prohibited.

Texas

Winery direct shipping permitted, up to 4 cases per year; retailer shipping prohibited.

Utah

Direct shipping prohibited.

Vermont

Winery direct shipping permitted, up to 12 cases per year; retailer shipping prohibited.

Virginia

Winery direct shipping permitted, up to 2 cases per month; retailer shipping permitted.

Washington

Winery direct shipping permitted; retailer shipping prohibited.

West Virginia

Winery direct shipping permitted, up to 2 cases per month; retailer shipping permitted.

Wisconsin

Winery direct shipping permitted, up to 12 cases per year; retailer shipping prohibited.

Wyoming

Winery direct shipping permitted, up to 2 cases per year; retailer shipping permitted.

Conclusion

Thanks to the internet, the barriers that previously existed to restrict access to wine manufacturers located across the globe have come down.

There have been many improvements to the transportation and logistics side of the industry that have made it accessible for anyone to import small amounts of wine at much lower shipping rates.

It also allows entrepreneurs the ability to benefit from the same wholesale prices that the larger importers have long enjoyed for years.

Please make sure you do your own research when it comes to being compliant with US regulations and take no short cuts.

To start importing your wines, you merely need to have your paperwork an order, a computer with stable internet access, your cell phone, a valid email, a home office address in your country, or a place to receive your wine, and a business plan.

That's literally all you need to get started.

Determine if you will choose to handle all of the logistics yourself or get a 3PL to help you. Do your homework to find the right partner to fulfill your orders.

In conclusion, here are a few key points:

- Don't be in too much of a rush. Patience is a virtue in the wine industry. Wait for inspiration to come to you and embrace it as it does.
- Do not wait until you have mastered everything to get started. Nothing is like business school, so get that out of your head.

- It costs virtually nothing to get started with this business. Are you going to need money eventually, yes, absolutely, but you do not need to know the entire picture from day 1.
- Take at least some time to do plenty of research as you go about starting out. Purchasing this book was just your first step.
- Start thinking of your brand and how you will shape that.
- Start creating your social media profiles; there is no cost associated with that.

Importing and exporting is a dazzling and spectacular world, yet it is also uniquely complex.

I sincerely hope this book has helped you on your entrepreneurial journey. If I have inspired you in any way, would you kindly consider leaving a review wherever you purchased this book?

Your feedback is vitally important to me, and I take it all to heart. Thank you in advance.

Congratulations to you, and best of luck in your new business venture!

Printed by Amazon Italia Logistica S.r.l.
Torrazza Piemonte (TO), Italy